BECKY'
SCHOOL OF THOUGHT

ANDREA BRADLEY
ZAC BEARD

Acknowledgement

Hope you enjoy 'Beckys School of Thought', thank you to Kelly Brown for proof reading and Robert Caffrey-Hill for proof reading and the foreword.

foreword

Dear Reader,

In this book, we will explore the importance of teaching children to think positively in negative scenarios. It is crucial for children to be able to reframe their thinking for healthy outcomes and develop the ability to navigate challenges and setbacks. This book provides techniques which will last a lifetime!

Through engaging stories and interactive exercises, we will empower children to embrace a growth mindset, build resilience, and develop problem-solving skills. By understanding how to approach negative situations with a positive attitude and a strategic mindset, children will be better equipped to overcome obstacles and thrive in an ever-changing world.

As you turn every page, remember that your mind is a beautiful garden. With attention and care, you can help it flourish and bloom. So take a deep breath, smile and let's embark on Becky's adventure together.

With love & positivity

Andrea & Zac

Fortune Telling

Becky could not sleep, the thought of school tomorrow was making her weep, she tossed and turned, situations running through her head,

the teachers, her friendship groups and the presentation filling her with dread.

Becky was predicting the future that she did not know. These negative thoughts she could not let go.

Mind Reading

Becky eventually slept but woke up late, she felt sad, anxious and tired with a lot on her plate.

The presentation in class was her main fear, picturing everyone laughing at her idea.

They will label her stupid and make fun, mind reading their thoughts is what Becky had done.

Negative Labelling

Arriving at school Becky sees Lily, she tells her how worried she is and asks

Lily replies 'That is a negative label you know, your presentation is great, and I am sure it will show.'

'Even if it goes wrong, it is all for the good as mistakes help you learn and grow through your childhood.'

Self-blaming

Becky is moody and does not respond, she thinks Lily has this all wrong.

Lily looks sad and wonders what she has done, but then realises that she is taking on Becky's projection.

When others feel rubbish their friendliness falls, but it is really nothing to do with us at all.

Catastrophizing

The bell rings for class, the butterflies grow. Becky is first to present and she cannot say NO!

She walks to the front and stands on the stage, everyone staring at her like a bird in a cage.

As she begins to talk her fears start to fade, this is not so bad, what a catastrophe she had made.

Loss of sleep and all that fear, If only Becky's positive thinking could have been more clear.

Setting The Bar Too High

After her presentation Becky returns to her seat, Lily is up next and rises to her feet.

Becky needs to listen to show respect, but her mind is still racing so she cannot connect.

Re-numerating over the one mistake she had made, she should have done better, when will these feelings fade?

Ignoring The Good

Lunchtime comes round with Becky still sad, Lily points out, 'You are just focusing on the bad.'

'You made one small error that only you know, no-one else would have noticed so just let it go!

When we ignore all the good that we have done, our heart sinks and stops us from having fun.

Black and White Thinking

**Extremes of black and white thinking then come into play,
thinking it is all wrong or all right with no area of grey**

**Whilst Lily is happy in the middle of these extremes,
Becky thinks she needs perfection to achieve her dreams!**

This type of thought pattern is not helpful at all,

you are not expected to be perfect at school.

Shoulding & Musting

Afternoon lessons resume at school, first up is volleyball in the hall.

With very long arms and feet that can hop, Becky thinks she SHOULD score highest and MUST come top.

Becky jumps far too high, she learns that shoulding and musting can sometimes lie.

As she strikes the ball, it hits the net, that top score just cannot be met. Becky feels embarrassed and full of shame, Lily reminds her that it's only a game!

Emotional Reasoning

At the end of the school day, Becky has learnt a lot, the worries she had in her mind she can now boycott.

Just because we think and feel something does not mean it is true, acquaintances like Lily can help you pull through.

Becky realised she had such a good friend,

Helping her change her thinking to a positive in the end!

Fortune telling

When we predict what is going to happen in the future with little or no evidence.

Talking points

1. What was Becky predicting?

2. How could Becky change her thinking to be more positive?

3. Have you ever worried about a future event? Did it turn out like you expected?

Fortune telling can create unnecessary worry and anxiety, thoughts of life events are often worse than the events themselves. If you find yourself predicting a negative future try changing your prediction to a positive. Think about all the times in the past you worried that something would happen but it didn't.

Mind Reading

When we think we know what someone else is thinking.

Talking points

1. What in the text tells you that Becky was mind reading?

2. How could Becky improve her confidence for her presentation?

3. Give examples of when you have experienced mind reading, how did it make you feel?

When we mind read it is what we are thinking not the other person, recognizing this and changing thoughts to a positive can change how you feel.

Negative labelling

When we attach a negative label to ourselves or others based on one characteristic of a person, not looking at the whole person.

Talking points

1. What negative label did Becky use?

2. Why should we not label ourselves or anyone else due to one situation?

3. What mistakes have you made that helped you grow?

Using negative labels can cement assumptions that you cannot do certain things in life. When we label someone else it can lower their self-confidence and self-belief.

Self-blaming

When we blame ourselves for how others behave or feel when we have done nothing wrong.

Talking points

1. Why do you think Lily thought she had done something to upset Becky?

2. How different are you with others when you are feeling happy compared to sad?

3. What could you do if your friend seems upset with you?

When we are not feeling great we can appear less friendly but it is not anything to do with anyone else, so if someone is unkind to you for no reason it is because they are unhappy and we should not blame ourselves.

Catastrophizing

When we blow things out of proportion, we make things seem far worse than they are.

Talking points

1. How is Becky catastrophizing?

2. What do you think happens to our body and our mind when we catastrophize?

3. How can we stop ourselves making a big deal out of something?

Normally when we catastrophize it is an initial reaction based on little thought, taking a breath and looking for the positives in a given situation can reduce any anxieties.

Setting the bar too high

Thinking that everything we do has to be perfect otherwise we are a failure.

Talking points

1. Why was Becky upset?

2. Do you think it is good to always get everything right?

3. How could Becky have made the negative feelings fade?

When we have high expectations of ourselves or others, we can set ourselves up for disappointment or feelings of failure. There is no such thing as perfect, only our idea of what perfect is to us. We learn the most from the mistakes that we make.

Ignoring the good

When we only focus on the negative in a situation, ignoring all the positives.

Talking points

1. What positives could Becky have been thinking about?

2. How did Lily help Becky?

3. Think of examples when you ignored the good, how did it make you feel? What could you have thought instead?

It's important to always look for 'good' in every situation. If there are any negatives then use these to grow, learn and develop, turning everything into a positive.

Black and White Thinking

When we think of people, thoughts or actions as all bad/imperfect or all good/perfect , there is no in-between or 'grey area'

Talking points

1. How do you think it feels to need to be 'perfect' all the time?

2. What does being-perfect mean to you?

3. Have you ever felt like you weren't good enough? Can you look at this differently now ?

When we see things as all good or all bad we put pressure on ourselves and others by setting high expectations which doesn't allow for mistakes and can lead to stress, anxiety and judgement. Changing our self-talk from 'always' and 'never' to 'sometimes' and 'maybe' can help us find a middle ground in our thinking.

Shoulding and Musting

Any statements that include 'should' or 'must' create undue pressure on yourself or others to perform at an expected standard.

Talking points

1. What standards was Becky setting for herself?

2. What could Becky have said instead?

3. How do you think Becky felt when she didn't meet her expectations?

Saying 'I should' or 'I must' can increase anxiety before an event and feelings of failure after an event if the 'shoulds' and 'musts' are not met, it's better to say, 'I am going to try my best' or 'I shall be ok whatever the outcome.'

Emotional Reasoning

When we think just because we feel something it means it is true.

Talking points

1. What negative feelings does Becky experience?

2. Can you name some positive and negative feelings?

3. Why do you think it's important to understand that sometimes we might feel something but it might not be true?

Emotional reasoning is commonly linked to anxiety and panic disorders, as it involves misinterpreting one's emotions, such as thinking, "I feel anxious, so I must be in danger." Recognizing that an emotion doesn't necessarily reflect reality enables you to seek evidence to support that feeling. For instance, if you feel anxious and interpret it as danger, you can look for actual evidence of danger.

AUTHOR

Andrea Bradley

Andrea Bradley BSc (Hons) is a dynamic professional residing in Worcestershire, England, balancing her career as a Cognitive Behavioural Therapist and a fitness instructor. A dedicated mother of three girls, Andreas aim is to improve mental wellbeing, self-esteem and self-acceptance for her clients starting at school age thus improving their life journey with techniques they can use forever. Andrea struggled with mental health issues and childhood trauma and would do anything to help others not endure the same fate or at least be equipped to face life challenges. Her passion for wanting others to experience a happier start in life is what inspired her debut book which delves into the cognitive distortions that many if not all of us experience in our lifetime.

Contact

acbcounselling50@gmail.com for Cognitive Behavourial Therapy.

ILLUSTRATOR

Zac Beard

Zac Beard is an Illustrator and designer based in Worcestershire, England, when creating the visuals for 'Becky's School of Thought' he looked at the charaters as a whole, making every decision precisely, relating her look and feel from Andreas depiction. Zac used water colour as his medium to mirror the child-like essence of Becky, drawing fast and loose to reflect the chaos of Becky's inner thoughts, while keeping everything uniform and perfectly designed. Zac has loved illustrating this book and has worked closely with Andrea to achieve what we think is a very special children's book that is like no other.

Contact

zacbbeard@gmail.com for Design and Illustation inquires

Printed in Great Britain
by Amazon